7

A YOUNG WORLD
TRIPPER BOOK

Created and edited by
DESMOND MARWOOD
Written by
EDWARD HOLMES
Illustrated by
BEN and STEPHANIE MANCHIPP

Prepared in consultation with
MAJ. M. G. DEWEY, Secretary of the British Show Jumping Association

in which Uncle George takes Tony and Anne on a trip to a . . .

Printed in Great Britain by Gilmour & Dean.

horse show

NELSON
YOUNG WORLD

Tony and Anne had seen show jumping on television, but this was the first time they had been to a horse show. "There is more to horse shows than just show jumping," Uncle George told them.

Uncle George was their favourite Uncle. He often took them on interesting trips, and he was a great believer in asking questions.

"If you don't ask questions, then there are lots of wonderful things you never get to know about," he said. So the twins always asked questions—and usually it was Uncle George who had to do the answering.

They got to the show ground early, because Uncle George was helping his friend, Mr Brown, who had a horse in the show. The twins had met Mr Brown before, for they had once made a trip to his farm. Mr Brown was a modern farmer, and he used tractors to do much of his work. However, he still had some grand old farm horses.

"Let's look around before it gets too crowded," said Uncle George. "The field with the fence round it is the show ring. Then there is that other field, at the side of the big field, which is called the collecting ring."

"What do they collect?" Anne wanted to know.

Uncle George laughed. "When the show is on, they collect people and horses there, so that they are ready when their turn comes. But that is not really what is meant," he explained. "The collecting ring is where the riders mount their horses, and ride them round to get them fully under control. This is called 'collecting' a horse, which means getting the horse obedient to the rider's instructions and aids.

"Where are the horses now?" Tony asked. "I'll show you," said Uncle George, and led them to where there were rows of canvas-backed shelters.

They could see horses looking out of these stables. As they watched, people began leading them out, and brushing them down. Soon people were coming and going carrying buckets and brushes, blankets and saddles. Bridles were being put onto the horse's heads, and saddles on their backs.

By now it was about an hour before the show was due to start, and some of the riders began to take their horses through from the stables to the collecting ring. By now two jumps had been put up in the collecting ring. Neither of them was very high, and the horses jumped them easily.

"When you walk or run," said Uncle George, "you just move one foot after the other, for you only have two legs. But a horse has four legs, and there are different ways he can move them. These are called the 'gaits' of a horse. The walk is the slowest gait, the feet of a walking horse move like the feet of two people, marching one behind the other, but half a pace out of step. The feet come down, one, two, three, four, in four-time.

"Trotting comes next, and that is in two-time," Uncle George went on, "see—that horse over there is trotting, and if you watch carefully, you will see that his feet are moving in pairs. The left front moves with the right hind, and, of course, the right front moves with the left hind. So when you ride a trotting horse, you can feel the pairs of hooves coming down in two-time, one, two, one, two."

"That horse isn't trotting—and he isn't going as fast as some that are," said Anne pointing. "He's cantering," replied Uncle George, "horses can canter very slowly, but they move their legs quite differently from trotting. Cantering is in three-time. First one hind hoof pushes off. Then the other hind hoof, and the opposite fore hoof hit the ground. Finally, the other fore hoof comes down alone."

"Galloping is the fastest gait," Uncle George went on. "Galloping is like cantering, but the horse strides out more powerfully. Galloping is three-time, too. And in a gallop, there is a moment when all four of a horse's hooves are off the ground, called the 'moment of suspension'. Of course, in both cantering and galloping, horses can 'push off' with either hind hoof. They are said to lead with whichever fore hoof lifts off first."

"Is it very hard to teach a horse to jump?" asked Tony. Uncle George shook his head. "Not really," he said, "because it is quite natural for a horse to jump. Watch—he canters up to the jump, and then, just before he reaches it, he checks slightly, so that his weight comes over his two hind hooves. Then he rears up at the front, and pushes off strongly with both hind hooves. This carries him up and over. You can see that if the jump is only a small one, he does not have to lift his body much."

"What he does have to do, though," Uncle George went on, " is to tuck his feet up well. Many a jump has been knocked down by a horse that trails his hooves. Coming down on the landing side, the horse stretches his forelegs in front of him, and lands on them striding, usually one just before the other. The best jumpers can clear over seven feet in a jump."

Then Uncle George went on to tell Tony and Anne what the parts of a horse are called.

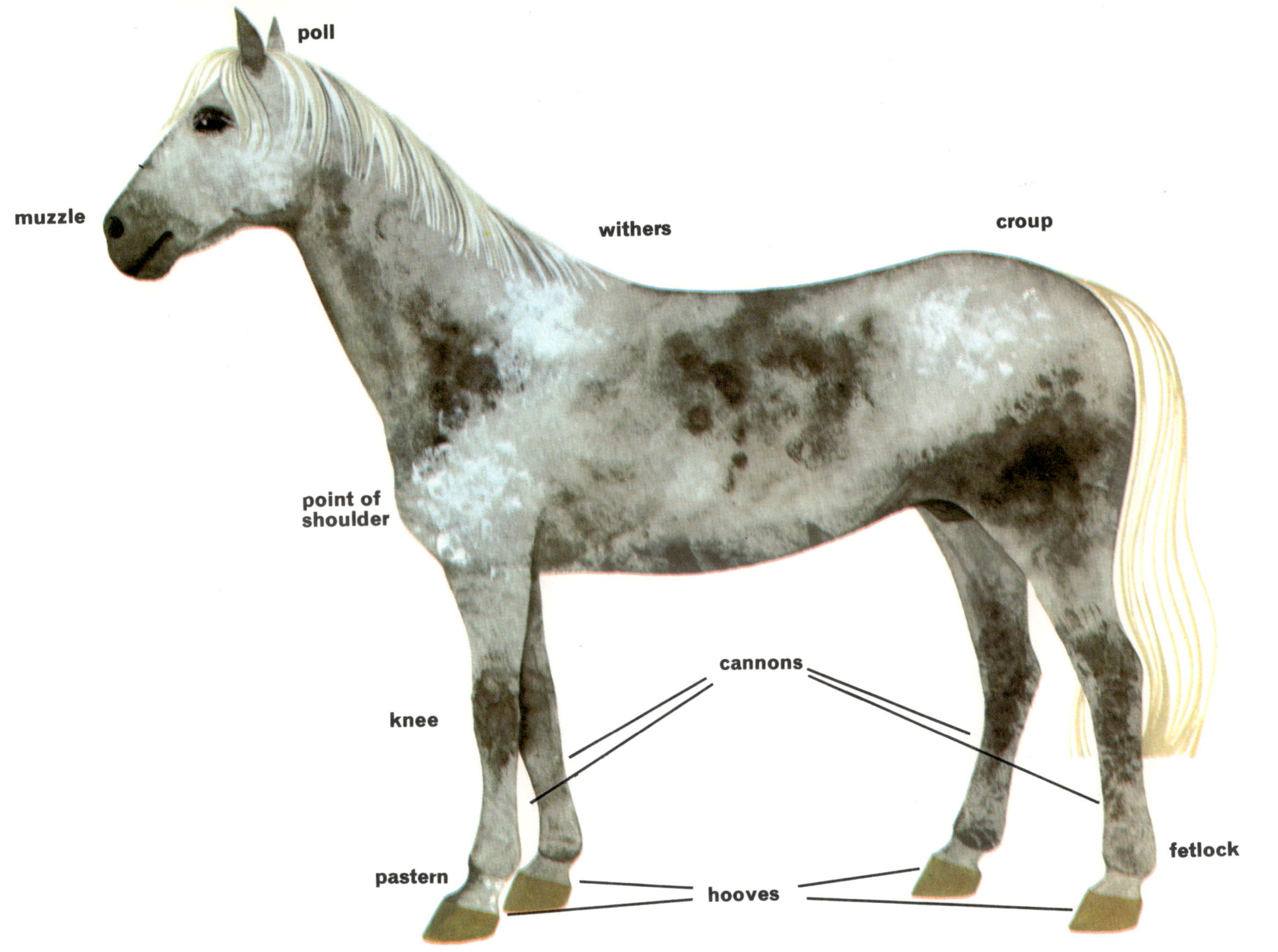
poll
muzzle
withers
croup
point of shoulder
cannons
knee
fetlock
pastern
hooves

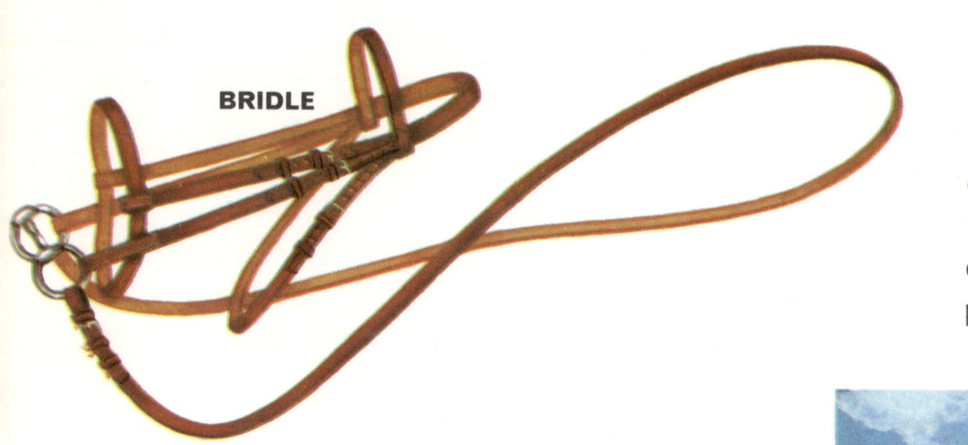

"Horses do look different when they are not wearing harness," said Anne. Uncle George shook his head. "What riding horses wear isn't called 'harness'," he explained. "It is called 'tack'. Harness is what a horse wears to pull a cart or a carriage. In fact, they used to call them 'harness horses', if their job was to pull things, rather than to carry riders."

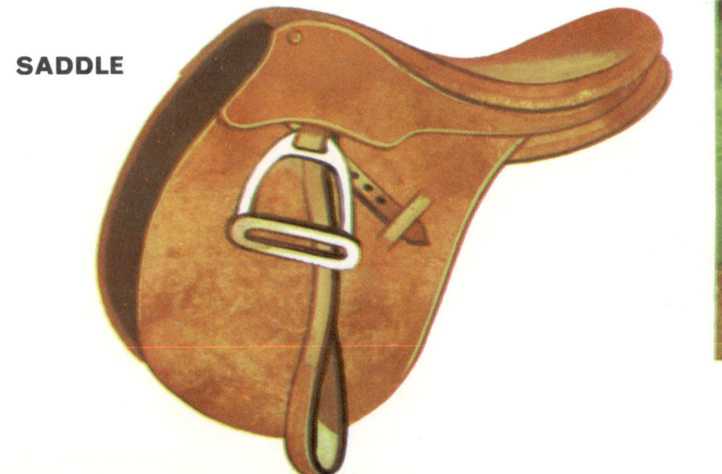

Uncle George explained what the parts of a horse's tack are called. Anne thought that the bit must feel very uncomfortable between a horse's teeth, but Uncle George said, "I don't think so. A horse has no teeth where the bit rests, only 'gums', which are called 'bars'."

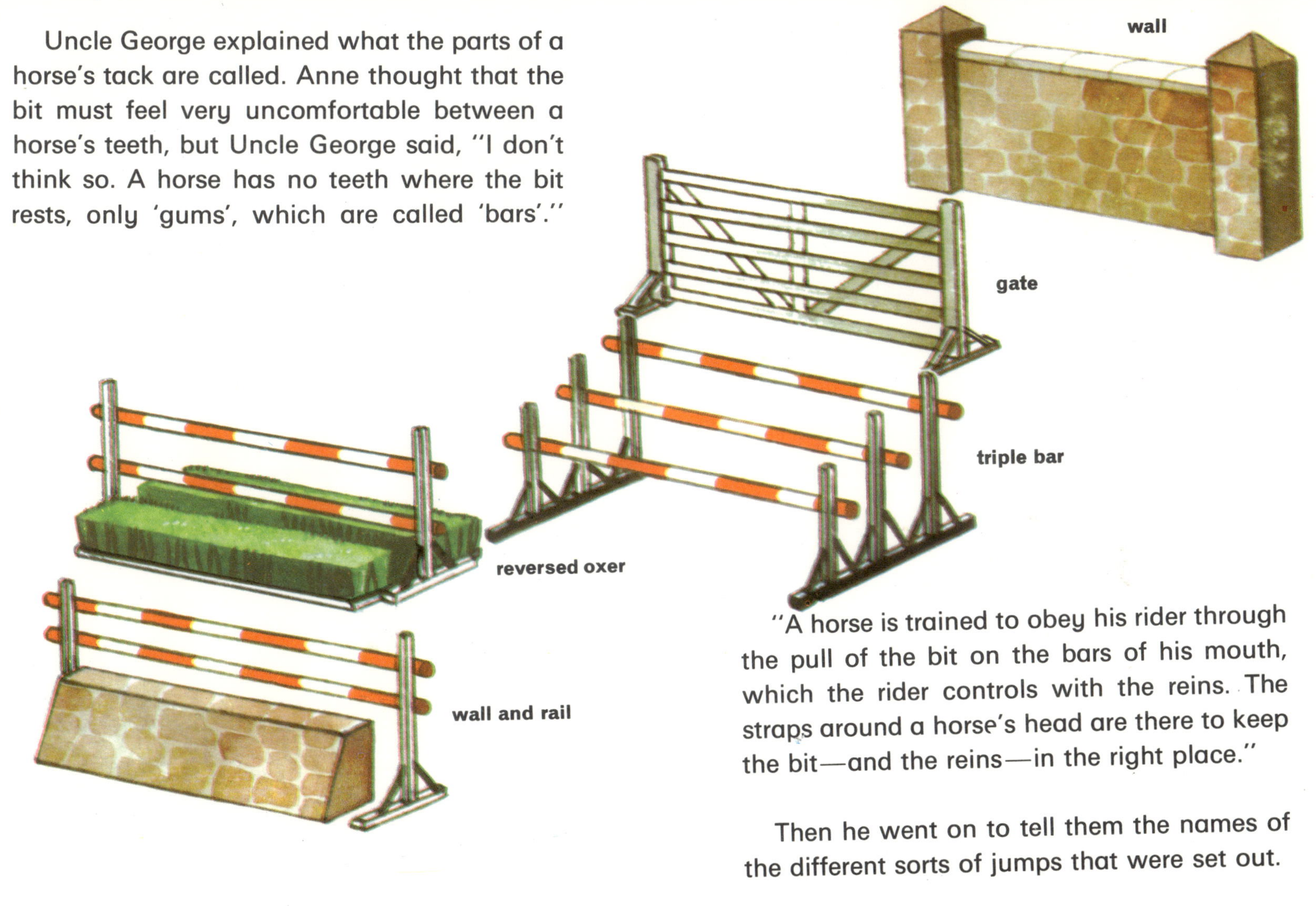

"A horse is trained to obey his rider through the pull of the bit on the bars of his mouth, which the rider controls with the reins. The straps around a horse's head are there to keep the bit—and the reins—in the right place."

Then he went on to tell them the names of the different sorts of jumps that were set out.

By now Tony and Anne were feeling quite expert, and they were easily picking out which horses were trotting, and which were cantering. "The riders don't pull very hard on the reins," said Tony. "No," Uncle George agreed, "the best riders control their horses by the lightest touch. Pulling hard spoils a horse's mouth." Uncle George paused, and pointed to a horse that was galloping. "See how that rider is using his heels on the horse's sides to urge it forwards."

Just then, some very different-looking horses appeared in the collecting ring. They wore fine trappings, and their riders were clad in colourful uniforms. "The show will be starting in a few minutes," said Uncle George, as they rode in, "Let's find ourselves a place . . ." They walked through to the stands which overlooked the main show-ring.

They had hardly got there, when the costumed riders trotted into the show-ring.

These were the heralds, opening the show in traditional manner. Some were carrying bugles, which they raised to their lips to play a fanfare. Some had big kettle drums, one on each side, on which they beat a tattoo.

Uncle George told the twins that these heralds were like the cavalry musicians who for centuries had taken part in pageants and Royal ceremonies.

"These horses are bigger than the others we've seen," said Anne, "are they a different sort?" "Yes," replied Uncle George, "they are not the sort of horses that would ordinarily be used for riding. They are more like the old-fashioned carriage horses." "I love big horses!" said Anne.

The heralds paraded right round the show ring. The big horses stepped proudly in time with the drum beats, and the shining bugles sounded fanfare after fanfare. The show had started!

"You're going to like this next event!" said Uncle George, grinning at Anne. Anne fixed her gaze on the ring entrance. Then she clapped her hands in delight, for in trotted a line of fine, big, horses, each led by a handler.

"Here comes the parade of heavy horses!" said Uncle George, "that big brown one is an old friend of mine. He belongs to Mr Brown. I groomed him this morning!"

"These big chaps are dying out, I'm sorry to say," Uncle George went on. "Once upon a time, they hauled all the heavy carts, and pulled ploughs for farmers. Now they are almost out of a job, for cars and tractors mostly do their work. The heavies are a separate race from the much lighter riding horses, and there are many different breeds. They all come from England and Western Europe."

"That brown horse that belongs to Mr Brown, is a Shire," said Uncle George, pointing. "Shires are the biggest breed of all horses. They can grow to measure nearly six feet at the withers. They are very gentle and willing, and one of the strongest animals in the world. One of them, working alone, can pull five tons, on the level. They move steadily—never very fast—and are very hard workers."

Uncle George pointed to another horse. "That's a Percheron, a French heavy," he said. "Percherons are not quite as tall as Shires, but they are just as powerful, and are said to have some Arab blood in their veins. Arabs are the light, fast horses from the lands to the south and east of the Mediterranean. That black horse is a Freisian, from Holland. That Gelderland horse is Dutch, too."

The heavies circled the ring, showing off their paces, and the judges inspected them.

Uncle George told them that the long hair covering their hooves was always called "feathers". Their hooves were huge! Mr Brown's Shire had hooves that were nearly the size of dinner plates!

Then the heavies went away, and in came the little chaps. "They are Shetland Ponies," explained Uncle George. "Ponies are horses that are smaller than fourteen hands and two inches—that's four foot, ten inches, measured at the withers. The Shetlands are the smallest pony breed of all, and though today they are mostly kept as pets for children, they once had to work very hard indeed for their living. They used to work in the low tunnels of coal mines, pulling trucks of coal. Shetland ponies are very strong. In fact, weight for weight, they are the strongest horses of all."

Next came the harness ponies. They were bigger ponies, but of much slimmer build than the tough, tiny Shetlands. They had to pull their "rigs" at a brisk, spanking trot, through a winding course marked out with obstacles.

It was a real test of skill for the drivers, and of skill and obedience for the lively little ponies.

The winner was the one who got round fastest, and knocked over the fewest obstacles.

There were more harness horses after the trotters, but this was a display, not a competition event. First into the ring came a bus—but it wasn't a motor-bus. "I never knew there were buses with horses!" exclaimed Tony.

"They were before your time!" laughed Uncle George, "before mine, too. They stopped running sixty years ago. My old Grandpa remembers them well. There were horse buses in London, and all the other big cities."

Next came a coach. "That's a stage-coach," said Uncle George. "It used to make the same sort of journies that long-distance motor coaches do now. At each stage of the journey, they would change the horses, at an Inn."

"They were very fast for their time—over a hundred years ago," he went on. "Some of them were even called 'Flying Machines" in those days. They could keep up a steady ten miles an hour, right from London to Dover."

The next event was the dressage competition. Tony and Anne had no idea what this meant, but when the first dressage rider appeared, Anne said brightly, "It's a fancy dress competition! Is that what dressage means?" Uncle George shook his head. "No—but the dress is very important. It is the old-fashioned dress, that people found best for riding in the days when everybody rode horses. But there's more to dressage than that. The object of the competition is to judge horse and rider on how they perform very difficult and exact movements. Watch this rider; you cannot see what she is doing to make her horse perform that lovely slow trot. That is because horse and rider are dressage trained."

"But what use is it?" asked Tony. "Nobody would ever ride a horse like that in the ordinary way." "True," agreed Uncle George, "but dressage training develops great skill in both horse and rider, and teaches the horse perfect obedience at all times. Dressage is the way to top-class riding of any sort."

Following the dressage came a display of High School Riding, in which the horses performed spectacular leaps and kicks.

"We saw this on our trip to the circus," said Tony. "That's right," replied Uncle George. "That's where it is usually seen nowadays. But once this sort of riding was a very serious business. Long ago, when knights wore armour, their horses were trained to do the leaps and kicks that are part of High School."

"Whatever for?" frowned Anne. "It was for fighting," said Uncle George. "The knight used his horse as a weapon."

There was an interval after the High School display, and Uncle George went off to help put up the jumps for the Show jumping competition, which was next. Tony began to show off his knowledge to Anne.

"The riders are given "faults" each time they knock a jump down, or when the horse refuses to jump," he said. "The rider with fewest faults is the winner." Of course, Anne knew that!

"They don't always do that," said Anne, determined not to be out-done. "If they get more than one rider with the same number of faults, they have a jump-off against the clock, and the rider who gets round in the shortest time wins." "Oh yes," replied Tony, "but faults still count, even when they are jumping against the clock!"

Uncle George came back then, and a few minutes later they were watching the show jumping. The competition was the final round of many other contests that had already been held by riding clubs and schools all over the county. The sixteen riders competing were the best from all these clubs and schools.

"This course is a real test for the riders." Said Uncle George, "It isn't just the jumps themselves that are difficult. They are spaced out so that the riders must pace their horses correctly. This takes a lot of skill."

After this contest, and when the winner had made his lap of honour, there was a 'puissance' competition. Six jumps were put out for this, and all but the first were big jumps.

"What's 'puissance'?" asked Anne. "'Puissance' is a word that means 'power'," Uncle George answered. "In a puissance contest, the winner is the horse that jumps highest."

Six out of the ten entrants had a clear first round. Now the jumps were reduced to four, but one, the wall, was made higher. After this, only two riders were left. The jumps were reduced to just a fence, and that wall, which was made higher still. Both riders had a clear round—and the wall was made even bigger. This time one rider just tipped off some of the top bricks, and a huge sigh went up from every single person watching!

They watched as the prizes were presented, and then they went home. And as Anne said, "I've seen show jumping on television before, but this really was the real thing!"

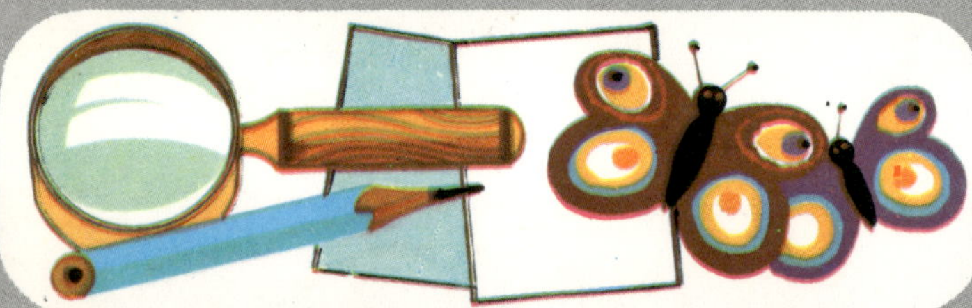

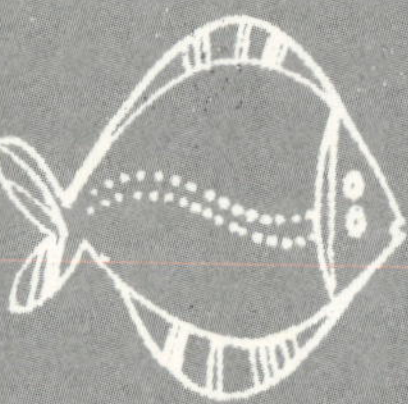